HUMA

ENCYCLICAL LET
BY DI

POPE LEO XIII

ON

Freemasonry

To Our Venerable Brethren, All Patriarchs, Primates, Archbishops and Bishops of the Catholic World,

In Grace and Communion with the Apostolic See, POPE LEO XIII

Venerable Brethren,

Health and Apostolic Benediction

Two Kingdoms

1. The race of man, after its miserable fall from God, the Creator and the Giver of heavenly gifts, "through the envy of the devil," separated into two diverse and opposite parts, of which the one steadfastly contends for truth and virtue, the other for those things which are contrary to virtue and to truth. The one is the kingdom of God on earth, namely, the true Church of Jesus Christ; and those who desire from their heart to be united with it, so as to gain salvation, must of necessity serve God and His only-begotten Son with their whole mind and with an entire will. The other is the kingdom of Satan, in whose possession and control are all whosoever follow the fatal example of their leader and of our first parents, those who refuse to obey the divine and eternal law, and who have many aims of their own in contempt of God, and many aims also against God.

Two Loves and Two Cities

2. This twofold kingdom St. Augustine keenly discerned and described after the manner of two cities, con-

Discussion Club Outline Copyrighted by The Missionary Society of St. Paul the Apostle in the State of New York, 1944.

trary in their laws because striving for contrary objects; and with a subtle brevity he expressed the efficient cause of each in these words: "Two loves formed two cities: the love of self, reaching even to contempt of God, an earthly city; and the love of God, reaching to contempt of self, a heavenly one." At every period of time each has been in conflict with the other, with a variety and multiplicity of weapons and of warfare, although not always with equal ardor and assault. At this period, however, the partisans of evil seem to be combining together, and to be struggling with united vehemence, led on or assisted by that strongly organized and widespread association called the Freemasons. No longer making any secret of their purposes, they are now boldly rising up against God Himself. They are planning the destruction of holy Church publicly and openly, and this with the set purpose of utterly despoiling the nations of Christendom, if it were possible, of the blessings obtained for us through Jesus Christ our Saviour. Lamenting these evils, We are constrained by the charity which urges Our heart to cry out often to God: "For lo, Thy enemies have made a noise; and they that hate Thee have lifted up the head. They have taken a malicious counsel against Thy people, and they have consulted against Thy saints. They have said, 'Come, and let us destroy them, so that they be not a nation.' "

The Pope's Duty

3. At so urgent a crisis, when so fierce and so pressing an onslaught is made upon the Christian name, it is Our office to point out the danger, to mark who are the adversaries, and to the best of Our power to make head against their plans and devices, that those may not perish whose salvation is committed to Us, and that the kingdom of Jesus Christ intrusted to Our charge may not only stand and remain whole, but may be enlarged by an ever-increasing growth throughout the world.

Our Predecessors on the Alert

4. The Roman Pontiffs Our predecessors, in their incessant watchfulness over the safety of the Christian people, were prompt in detecting the presence and the purpose of this capital enemy immediately it sprang into the light instead of hiding as a dark conspiracy; and moreover they

took occasion with true foresight to give, as it were, the alarm, and to admonish both princes and nations to stand on their guard, and not allow themselves to be caught by the devices and snares laid out to deceive them.

From Clement XII to Pius IX

5. The first warning of the danger was given by Clement XII in the year 1738, and his Constitution was confirmed and renewed by Benedict XIV. Pius VII followed the same path; and Leo XII, by his Apostolic Constitution, *"Quo graviora,"* put together the acts and decrees of former Pontiffs on this subject, and ratified and confirmed them forever. In the same sense spoke Pius VIII, Gregory XVI, and many times over Pius IX.

The Church, the State and Masonry

6. For as soon as the constitution and the spirit of the Masonic sect were clearly discovered by manifest signs of its actions, by cases investigated, by the publication of its laws, and of its rites and commentaries, with the addition often of the personal testimony of those who were in the secret, this Apostolic See denounced the sect of the Freemasons, and publicly declared its constitution, as contrary to law and right, to be pernicious no less to Christendom than to the State; and it forbade any one to enter the society, under the penalties which the Church is wont to inflict upon exceptionally guilty persons. The sectaries, indignant at this, thinking to elude or to weaken the force of these decrees, partly by contempt of them, and partly by calumny, accused the Sovereign Pontiffs who had passed them either of exceeding the bounds of moderation in their decrees or of decreeing what was not just. This was the manner in which they endeavored to elude the authority and the weight of the Apostolic Constitutions of Clement XII and Benedict XIV, as well as of Pius VII and Pius IX. Yet in the very society itself there were to be found men who unwillingly acknowledged that the Roman Pontiffs had acted within their right, according to the Catholic doctrine and discipline. The Pontiffs received the same assent, and in strong terms, from many princes and heads of governments, who made it their business either to delate the Masonic society to the Apostolic See, or of their own accord by special enactments to brand it as pernicious, as, for

example, in Holland, Austria, Switzerland, Spai., Bavaria, Savoy, and other parts of Italy.

Our Predecessors' Warnings Vindicated

7. But, what is of highest importance, the course of events has demonstrated the prudence of Our predecessors. For their provident and paternal solicitude had not always and everywhere the result desired; and this, either because of the simulation and cunning of some who were active agents in the mischief, or else of the thoughtless levity of the rest who ought, in their own interest, to have given to the matter their diligent attention. In consequence the sect of Freemasons grew with a rapidity beyond conception in the course of a century and a half, until it came to be able, by means of fraud or of audacity, to gain such entrance into every rank of the State as to seem to be almost its ruling power. This swift and formidable advance has brought upon the Church, upon the power of princes, upon the public well-being, precisely that grievous harm which Our predecessors had long before foreseen. Such a condition has been reached that henceforth there will be grave reason to fear, not indeed for the Church—for her foundation is much too firm to be overturned by the effort of men—but for those States in which prevails the power, either of the sect of which we are speaking or of other sects not dissimilar which lend themselves to it as disciples and subordinates.

The Teaching and Aims of Masonry

8. For these reasons We no sooner came to the helm of the Church than We clearly saw and felt it to be Our duty to use Our authority to the very utmost against so vast an evil. We have several times already, as occasion served, attacked certain chief points of teaching which showed in a special manner the perverse influence of Masonic opinions. Thus, in Our Encyclical Letter, *"Quod Apostolici muneris,"* We endeavored to refute the monstrous doctrines of the Socialists and Communists; afterwards, in another beginning *"Arcanum,"* We took pains to defend and explain the true and genuine idea of domestic life, of which marriage is the spring and origin; and again, in that which begins *"Diuturnum,"* We described the ideal of political government conformed to the principles of Christian wisdom,

[4]

which is marvelously in harmony, on the one hand, with the natural order of things, and, on the other, with the well-being of both sovereign princes and of nations. It is now Our intention, following the example of Our predecessors, directly to treat of the Masonic society itself, of its whole teaching, of its aims, and of its manner of thinking and acting, in order to bring more and more into the light its power for evil, and to do what We can to arrest the contagion of this fatal plague.

Unity of All Secret Societies

9. There are several organized bodies which, though differing in name, in ceremonial, in form and origin, are nevertheless so bound together by community of purpose and by the similarity of their main opinions, as to make in fact one thing with the sect of the Freemasons, which is a kind of center whence they all go forth, and whither they all return. Now, these no longer show a desire to remain concealed; for they hold their meetings in the daylight and before the public eye, and publish their own newspaper organs; and yet, when thoroughly understood, they are found still to retain the nature and the habits of secret societies. There are many things like mysteries which it is the fixed rule to hide with extreme care, not only from strangers, but from very many members also; such as their secret and final designs, the names of the chief leaders, and certain secret and inner meetings, as well as their decisions, and the ways and means of carrying them out. This is, no doubt, the object of the manifold difference among the members as to right, office, and privilege—of the received distinction of orders and grades, and of that severe discipline which is maintained.

Secrecy and Deceit

Candidates are generally commanded to promise—nay, with a special oath, to swear—that they will never, to any person, at any time or in any way, make known the members, the passes, or the subjects discussed. Thus, with a fraudulent external appearance, and with a style of simulation which is always the same, the Freemasons, like the Manichees of old, strive, as far as possible, to conceal themselves, and to admit no witnesses but their own members. As a convenient manner of concealment, they assume the character of literary men and scholars associated for purposes of learning. They speak of their zeal for a more cultured refinement, and of their love for the poor; and they declare their one wish to be the amelioration of the condition of the masses, and to share with the largest possible number all the benefits of civil life. Were these purposes aimed at in real truth, they are by no means the whole of their object. Moreover, to be enrolled, it is necessary that the candidates promise and undertake to be thenceforward strictly obedient to their leaders and masters with the utmost submission and fidelity, and to be in readiness to do their bidding upon the slightest expression of their will; or, if disobedient, to submit to the direst penalties and death itself. As a fact, if any are judged to have betrayed the doings of the sect or to have resisted commands given, punishment is inflicted on them not infrequently, and with so much audacity and dexterity that the assassin very often escapes the detection and penalty of his crime.

Evil Fruits of Masonry

10. But to simulate and wish to lie hid; to bind men like slaves in the very tightest bonds, and without giving any sufficient reason; to make use of men enslaved to the will of another for any arbitrary act; to arm men's right hands for bloodshed after securing impunity for the crime—all this is an enormity from which nature recoils. Wherefore reason and truth itself make it plain that the society of which we are speaking is in antagonism with justice and natural uprightness. And this becomes still plainer, inasmuch as other arguments also, and those very manifest, prove that it is essentially opposed to natural virtue. For, no matter how great may be men's cleverness in concealing and their experience in lying, it is impossible to prevent the effects of any cause from showing, in some way, the intrinsic nature of the cause whence they come. "A good tree cannot produce bad fruit, nor a bad tree produce good fruit." Now, the Masonic sect produces fruits that are pernicious and of the bitterest savor. For, from what We have above most clearly shown, that which is their ultimate purpose forces itself into view—namely, the utter overthrow of that whole religious and political order of the world which the Christian teaching has produced, and the substitution of a new state of things

in accordance with their ideas, of which the foundations and laws shall be drawn from mere "Naturalism."

Masonry and Associated Organizations

11. What We have said, and are about to say, must be understood of the sect of the Freemasons taken generically, and in so far as it comprises the associations kindred to it and confederated with it, but not of the individual members of them. There may be persons amongst these, and not a few, who, although not free from the guilt of having entangled themselves in such associations, yet are neither themselves partners in their criminal acts, nor aware of the ultimate object which they are endeavoring to attain. In the same way, some of the affiliated societies, perhaps, by no means approve of the extreme conclusions which they would, if consistent, embrace as necessarily following from their common principles, did not their very foulness strike them with horror. Some of these, again, are led by circumstances of times and places either to aim at smaller things than the others usually attempt, or than they themselves would wish to attempt. They are not, however, for this reason, to be reckoned as alien to the Masonic federation; for the Masonic federation is to be judged not so much by the things which it has done, or brought to completion, as by the sum of its pronounced opinions.

The Principles of Naturism

12. Now, the fundamental doctrine of the Naturalists, which they sufficiently make known by their very name, is that human nature and human reason ought in all things to be mistress and guide. Laying this down, they care little for duties to God, or pervert them by erroneous and vague opinions. For they deny that anything has been taught by God; they allow no dogma of religion or truth which cannot be understood by the human intelligence, nor any teacher who ought to be believed by reason of his authority. And since it is the special and exclusive duty of the Catholic Church fully to set forth in words truths divinely received, to teach, besides other divine helps to salvation, the authority of its office, and to defend the same with perfect purity, it is against the Church that the rage and attack of the enemies are principally directed.

Masonry Upholds Naturalism

13. In those matters which regard religion let it be seen how the sect of the Freemasons acts, especially where it is more free to act without restraint, and then let any one judge whether in fact it does not wish to carry out the policy of the Naturalists. By a long and persevering labor, they endeavor to bring about this result—namely, that the office and authority of the Church may become of no account in the civil State; and for this same reason they declare to the people and contend that Church and State ought to be altogether disunited. By this means they reject from the laws and from the commonwealth the wholesome influence of the Catholic religion; and they consequently imagine that States ought to be constituted without any regard for the laws and precepts of the Church.

Masonry Attacks Christ's Church

14. Nor do they think it enough to disregard the Church—the best of guides—unless they also injure it by their hostility. Indeed, with them it is lawful to attack with impunity the very foundations of the Catholic religion, in speech, in writing, and in teaching; and even the rights of the Church are not spared, and the offices with which it is divinely invested are not safe. The least possible liberty to manage affairs is left to the Church; and this is done by laws not apparently very hostile, but in reality framed and fitted to hinder freedom of action. Moreover, We see exceptional and onerous laws imposed upon the clergy, to the end that they may be continually diminished in number and in necessary means. We see also the remnants of the possessions of the Church fettered by the strictest conditions, and subjected to the power and arbitrary will of the administrators of the State, and the religious orders rooted up and scattered.

Masonry Assails Christ's Vicar

15. But against the Apostolic See and the Roman Pontiff the contention of these enemies has been for a long time directed. The Pontiff was first, for specious reasons, thrust out from the bulwark of his liberty and of his right, the civil princedom; soon he was unjustly driven into a condition which was unbearable because of the difficulties raised on

all sides; and now the time has come when the partisans of the sects openly declare, what in secret among themselves they have for a long time plotted, that the sacred power of the Pontiffs must be abolished, and that the Pontificate itself, founded by divine right, must be utterly destroyed. If other proofs were wanting, this fact would be sufficiently disclosed by the testimony of men well informed, of whom some at other times, and others again recently, have declared it to be true of the Freemasons that they especially desire to assail the Church with irreconcilable hostility, and that they will never rest until they have destroyed whatever the supreme Pontiffs have established for the sake of religion.

Masonry Undermines All Religion

16. If those who are admitted as members are not commanded to abjure by any form of words the Catholic doctrines, this omission, so far from being adverse to the designs of the Freemasons, is more useful for their purposes. First, in this way they easily deceive the simple-minded and the heedless, and can induce a far greater number to become members. Again, as all who offer themselves are received whatever may be their form of religion, they thereby teach the great error of this age—that a regard for religion should be held as an indifferent matter, and that all religions are alike. This manner of reasoning is calculated to bring about the ruin of all forms of religion, and especially of the Catholic religion, which, as it is the only one that is true, cannot, without great injustice, be regarded as merely equal to other religions.

Masonic Belief in God

17. But the Naturalists go much further; for having, in the highest things, entered upon a wholly erroneous course, they are carried headlong to extremes, either by reason of the weakness of human nature, or because God inflicts upon them the just punishment of their pride. Hence it happens that they no longer consider as certain and permanent those things which are fully understood by the natural light of reason, such as certainly are—the existence of God, the immaterial nature of the human soul, and its immortality. The sect of the Freemasons, by a similar course of error, is exposed to these same dangers; for although in a general

way they may profess the existence of God, they themselves are witnesses that they do not all maintain this truth with the full assent of the mind or with a firm conviction. Neither do they conceal that this question about God is the greatest source and cause of discords among them; in fact, it is certain that a considerable contention about this same subject has existed among them very lately. But indeed the sect allows great liberty to its votaries, so that to each side is given the right to defend its own opinion, either that there is a God, or that there is none; and those who obstinately contend that there is no God are as easily initiated as those who contend that God exists, though, like the Pantheists, they have false notions concerning Him: all which is nothing else than taking away the reality, while retaining some absurd representation of the divine nature.

Loss of Natural Truths

18. When this greatest fundamental truth has been overturned or weakened, it follows that those truths also which are known by the teaching of nature must begin to fall—namely, that all things were made by the free will of God the Creator; that the world is governed by Providence; that souls do not die; that to this life of men upon the earth there will succeed another and an everlasting life.

Effect on Morality

19. When these truths are done away with, which are as the principles of nature and important for knowledge and for practical use, it is easy to see what will become of both public and private morality. We say nothing of those more heavenly virtues, which no one can exercise or even acquire without a special gift and grace of God; of which necessarily no trace can be found in those who reject as unknown the redemption of mankind, the grace of God, the sacraments, and the happiness to be obtained in heaven. We speak now of the duties which have their origin in natural probity. That God is the Creator of the world and its provident Ruler; that the eternal law commands the natural order to be maintained, and forbids that it be disturbed; that the last end of men is a destiny far above human things and beyond this sojourning upon the earth: these are the sources and these the principles of all justice and morality.

No Foundation for Justice

If these be taken away, as the Naturalists and Freemasons desire, there will immediately be no knowledge as to what constitutes justice and injustice, or upon what principle morality is founded. And, in truth, the teaching of morality which alone finds favor with the sect of Freemasons, and in which they contend that youth should be instructed, is that which they call "civil," and "independent," and "free," namely, that which does not contain any religious belief. But how insufficient such teaching is, how wanting in soundness, and how easily moved by every impulse of passion, is sufficiently proved by its sad fruits, which have already begun to appear. For wherever, by removing Christian education, the sect has begun more completely to rule, there goodness and integrity of morals have begun quickly to perish, monstrous and shameful opinions have grown up, and the audacity of evil deeds has risen to a high degree. All this is commonly complained of and deplored; and not a few of those who by no means wish to do so are compelled by abundant evidence to give not infrequently the same testimony.

Weakness of Our Nature

20. Moreover, human nature was stained by original sin, and is therefore more disposed to vice than to virtue. For a virtuous life it is absolutely necessary to restrain the disorderly movements of the soul, and to make the passions obedient to reason. In this conflict human things must very often be despised, and the greatest labors and hardships must be undergone, in order that reason may always hold its sway. But the Naturalists and Freemasons, having no faith in those things which we have learned by the revelation of God, deny that our first parents sinned, and consequently think that free will is not at all weakened and inclined to evil. On the contrary, exaggerating rather our natural virtue and excellence and placing therein alone the principle and rule of justice, they cannot even imagine that there is any need at all of a constant struggle and a perfect steadfastness to overcome the violence and rule of our passions.

A Gospel of Pleasure

Wherefore we see that men are publicly tempted by the many allurements of pleasure; that there are journals and pamphlets with neither moderation nor shame; that stage-plays are remarkable for license; that designs for works of art are shamelessly sought in the laws of a so-called *realism;* that the contrivances of a soft and delicate life are most carefully devised; and that all the blandishments of pleasure are diligently sought out by which virtue may be lulled to sleep. Wickedly also, but at the same time quite consistently, do those act who do away with the expectation of the joys of heaven, and bring down all happiness to the level of mortality, and, as it were, sink it in the earth. Of what We have said the following fact, astonishing not so much in itself as in its open expression, may serve as a confirmation. For since generally no one is accustomed to obey crafty and clever men so submissively as those whose soul is weakened and broken down by the domination of the passions, there have been in the sect of the Freemasons some who have plainly determined and proposed that, artfully and of set purpose, the multitude should be satiated with a boundless license of vice, as, when this had been done, it would easily come under their power and authority for any acts of daring.

Teachings on Marriage

21. What refers to domestic life in the teaching of the Naturalists is almost all contained in the following declarations. That marriage belongs to the genus of commercial contracts, which can rightly be revoked by the will of those who made them, and that the civil rulers of the State have power over the matrimonial bond; that in the education of youth nothing is to be taught in the matter of religion as of certain and fixed opinion; and each one must be left at liberty to follow, when he comes of age, whatever he may prefer. To these things the Freemasons fully assent; and not only assent, but have long endeavored to make them into a law and institution. For in many countries, and those nominally Catholic, it is enacted that no marriages shall be considered lawful except those contracted by the civil rite; in other places the law permits divorce; and in others every effort is used to make it lawful as soon as may be. Thus the time is quickly coming when marriages will be turned into another kind of contract—that is, into changeable and uncertain unions which fancy may join together, and which the same when changed may disunite.

Educational Principles

With the greatest unanimity the sect of the Freemasons also endeavors to take to itself the education of youth. They think that they can easily mold to their opinions that soft and pliant age, and bend it whither they will; and that nothing can be more fitted than this to enable them to bring up the youth of the State after their own plan. Therefore in the education and instruction of children they allow no share, either of teaching or of discipline, to the ministers of the Church; and in many places they have procured that the education of youth shall be exclusively in the hands of laymen, and that nothing which treats of the most important and most holy duties of men to God shall be introduced into the instructions on morals.

Political Doctrines

22. Then come their doctrines of politics, in which the Naturalists lay down that all men have the same right, and are in every respect of equal and like condition; that each one is naturally free; that no one has the right to command another; that it is an act of violence to require men to obey any authority other than that which is obtained from themselves. According to this, therefore, all things belong to the free people; power is held by the command or permission of the people, so that, when the popular will changes, rulers may lawfully be deposed; and the source of all rights and civil duties is either in the multitude or in the governing authority when this is constituted according to the latest doctrines. It is held also that the State should be without God; that in the various forms of religion there is no reason why one should have precedence of another; and that they are all to occupy the same place.

Communism the Sequel

23. That these doctrines are equally acceptable to the Freemasons, and that they would wish to constitute States according to this example and model, is too well known to require proof. For some time past they have openly endeavored to bring this about with all their strength and resources; and in this they prepare the way for not a few bolder men who are hurrying on even to worse things, in their endeavor to obtain equality and community of all goods by the destruction of every distinction of rank and property.

24. What therefore the sect of the Freemasons is, and what course it pursues, appears sufficiently from the summary We have briefly given. Their chief dogmas are so greatly and manifestly at variance with reason, that nothing can be more perverse. To wish to destroy the religion and the Church which God Himself has established, and whose perpetuity He insures by His protection, and to bring back after a lapse of eighteen centuries the manners and customs of the pagans, is signal folly and audacious impiety. Neither is it less horrible nor more tolerable that they should repudiate the benefits which Jesus Christ has mercifully obtained, not only for individuals, but also for the family and for civil society, benefits which, even according to the judgment and testimony of enemies of Christianity, are very great. In this insane and wicked endeavor we may almost see the implacable hatred and spirit of revenge with which Satan himself is inflamed against Jesus Christ.— So also the studious endeavor of the Freemasons to destroy the chief foundations of justice and honesty, and to co-operate with those who would wish, as if they were mere animals, to do what they please, tends only to the ignominious and disgraceful ruin of the human race.

Dangers to Society

The evil, too, is increased by the dangers which threaten both domestic and civil society. As We have elsewhere shown, in marriage, according to the belief of almost every nation, there is something sacred and religious; and the law of God has determined that marriages shall not be dissolved. If they are deprived of their sacred character, and made dissoluble, trouble and confusion in the family will be the result, the wife being deprived of her dignity and the children left without protection as to their interests and well-being.—To have in public matters no care for religion, and in the arrangement and administration of civil affairs to have no more regard for God than if He did not exist, is a rashness unknown to the very pagans; for in their heart and soul the notion of a divinity and the need of public religion were so firmly fixed that they would have thought it easier to have a city without foundation than a city without God. Human society, indeed, for which by nature we are formed, has been constituted by God the Author of nature; and from Him, as from their principle and source, flow in all their strength and permanence the countless benefits with which society abounds. As we are each of us admonished by the very voice of nature to worship God in piety and holiness, as the Giver unto us of life and of all that is good therein, so also and for the same reason, nations and States are bound to worship Him; and therefore it is clear that those who would absolve society from all religious duty act not only unjustly but also with ignorance and folly.

Foundation of Civic Obedience

25. As men are by the will of God born for civil union and society, and as the power to rule is so necessary a bond of society that, if it be taken away, society must at once be broken up, it follows that from Him Who is the Author of society has come also the authority to rule; so that whosoever rules, he is the minister of God. Wherefore, as the end and nature of human society so requires, it is right to obey the just commands of lawful authority, as it is right to obey God Who ruleth all things; and it is most untrue that the people have it in their power to cast aside their obedience whensoever they please.

True and False Equality

26. In like manner, no one doubts that all men are equal one to another, so far as regards their common origin and nature, or the last end which each one has to attain, or the rights and duties which are thence derived. But as the abilities of all are not equal, as one differs from another in the powers of mind or body, and as there are very many dissimilarities of manner, disposition, and character, it is most repugnant to reason to endeavor to confine all within the same measure, and to extend complete equality to the institutions of civil life. Just as a perfect condition of the body results from the conjunction and composition of its various members, which, though differing in form and purpose, make, by their union and the distribution of each one to its proper place, a combination beautiful to behold, firm in strength, and necessary for use; so, in the commonwealth, there is an almost infinite dissimilarity of men, as parts of the whole. If they are to be all equal, and each is to follow his own will, the State will appear most deformed; but if,

with a distinction of degrees of dignity, of pursuits and employments, all aptly conspire for the common good, they will present a natural image of a well-constituted State.

A Threat to States

27. Now, from the disturbing errors which We have described the greatest dangers to States are to be feared. For, the fear of God and reverence for divine laws being taken away, the authority of rulers despised, sedition permitted and approved, and the popular passions urged on to lawlessness, with no restraint save that of punishment, a change and overthrow of all things will necessarily follow. Yea, this change and overthrow is deliberately planned and put forward by many associations of *Communists* and *Socialists*; and to their undertakings the sect of Freemasons is not hostile, but greatly favors their designs, and holds in common with them their chief opinions. And if these men do not at once and everywhere endeavor to carry out their extreme views, it is not to be attributed to their teaching and their will, but to the virtue of that divine religion which cannot be destroyed; and also because the sounder part of men, refusing to be enslaved to secret societies, vigorously resist their insane attempts.

People and Rulers Deceived

28. Would that all men would judge of the tree by its fruits, and would acknowledge the seed and origin of the evils which press upon us, and of the dangers that are impending! We have to deal with a deceitful and crafty enemy, who, gratifying the ears of people and of princes, has ensnared them by smooth speeches and by adulation. Ingratiating themselves with rulers under a pretense of friendship, the Freemasons have endeavored to make them their allies and powerful helpers for the destruction of the Christian name; and that they might more strongly urge them on, they have, with determined calumny, accused the Church of invidiously contending with rulers in matters that affect their authority and sovereign power. Having, by these artifices, insured their own safety and audacity, they have begun to exercise great weight in the government of States; but nevertheless they are prepared to shake the foundations of empires, to harass the rulers of the State, to accuse, and to cast them out, as often as they appear to govern other-

wise than they themselves could have wished. In like manner they have by flattery deluded the people. Proclaiming with a loud voice liberty and public prosperity, and saying that it was owing to the Church and to sovereigns that the multitude were not drawn out of their unjust servitude and poverty, they have imposed upon the people; and, exciting them by a thirst for novelty, they have urged them to assail both the Church and the civil power. Nevertheless, the expectation of the benefits which were hoped for was greater than the reality; indeed, the common people, more oppressed than they were before, are deprived in their misery of that solace which, if things had been arranged in a Christian manner, they would have had with ease and in abundance. But whoever strive against the order which divine Providence has constituted pay usually the penalty of their pride, and meet with affliction and misery where they rashly hoped to find all things prosperous and in conformity with their desires.

Benefit of Church's Teaching

29. The Church, if she directs men to render obedience chiefly and above all to God the sovereign Lord, is wrongly and falsely believed either to be envious of the civil power or to arrogate to herself something of the rights of sovereigns. On the contrary, she teaches that what is rightly due to the civil power must be rendered to it with a conviction and consciousness of duty. In teaching that from God Himself comes the right of ruling, she adds a great dignity to civil authority, and no small help towards obtaining the obedience and good-will of the citizens. The friend of peace and sustainer of concord, she embraces all with maternal love; and, intent only upon giving help to mortal man, she teaches that to justice must be joined clemency, equity to authority, and moderation to law-giving; that no one's right must be violated; that order and public tranquillity are to be maintained; and that the poverty of those who are in need is, as far as possible, to be relieved by public and private charity. "But for this reason," to use the words of St. Augustine, "men think, or would have it believed, that Christian teaching is not suited to the good of the State; for they wish the State to be founded not on solid virtue, but on the impunity of vice." Knowing these things, both princes and people would act with political wisdom, and according to the needs

of general safety, if, instead of joining with Freemasons to destroy the Church, they joined with the Church in repelling their attacks.

The Popes' Warning Reiterated

30. Whatever the future may be, in this grave and widespread evil it is Our duty, Venerable Brethren, to endeavor to find a remedy. And because We know that Our best and firmest hope of a remedy is in the power of that divine religion which the Freemasons hate in proportion to their fear of it, We think it to be of chief importance to call that most saving power to Our aid against the common enemy. Therefore, whatsoever the Roman Pontiffs Our predecessors have decreed for the purpose of opposing the undertakings and endeavors of the Masonic sect, and whatsoever they have enacted to deter or withdraw men from societies of this kind, We ratify and confirm it all by Our Apostolic authority: and trusting greatly to the good-will of Christians, We pray and beseech each one, for the sake of his eternal salvation, to be most conscientiously careful not in the least to depart from what the Apostolic See has commanded in this matter.

No Compromise With Masonry

31. We pray and beseech you, Venerable Brethren, to join your efforts with Ours, and earnestly to strive for the extirpation of this foul plague, which is creeping through the veins of the State. You have to defend the glory of God and the salvation of your neighbor; and with this object of your strife before you, neither courage nor strength will be wanting. It will be for your prudence to judge by what means you can best overcome the difficulties and obstacles you meet with. But as it befits the authority of Our office that We Ourselves should point out some suitable way of proceeding, We wish it to be your rule first of all to tear away the mask from Freemasonry, and to let it be seen as it really is; and by sermons and Pastoral Letters to instruct the people as to the artifices used by societies of this kind in seducing men and enticing them into their ranks, and as to the depravity of their opinions and the wickedness of their acts. As Our predecessors have many times repeated, let no man think that he may for any reason whatsoever join the Masonic sect, if he values his Catholic

name and his eternal salvation as he ought to value them. Let no one be deceived by a pretense of honesty. It may seem to some that Freemasons demand nothing that is openly contrary to religion and morality; but, as the whole principle and object of the sect lies in what is vicious and criminal, to join with these men or in any way to help them cannot be lawful.

Sound Religious Instruction Needed

32. Further, by assiduous teaching and exhortation, the multitude must be drawn to learn diligently the precepts of religion; for which purpose We earnestly advise that by opportune writings and sermons they be taught the elements of those sacred truths in which Christian philosophy is contained. The result of this will be that the minds of men will be made sound by instruction, and will be protected against many forms of error and inducements to wickedness, especially in the present unbounded freedom of writing and insatiable eagerness for learning.

United Effort of Clergy and Laity

33. Great, indeed, is the work; but in it the clergy will share your labors, if, through your care, they are fitted for it by learning and a well-trained life. This good and great work requires to be helped also by the industry of those amongst the laity in whom a love of religion and of country is joined to learning and goodness of life. By uniting the efforts of both clergy and laity, strive, Venerable Brethren, to make men thoroughly know and love the Church; for the greater their knowledge and love of the Church, the more will they be turned away from clandestine societies.

Ideal of St. Francis

34. Wherefore, not without cause do We use this occasion to state again what We have stated elsewhere, namely, that the Third Order of St. Francis, whose discipline We a little while ago prudently mitigated, should be studiously promoted and sustained: for the whole object of this Order, as constituted by its founder, is to invite men to an imitation of Jesus Christ, to a love of the Church, and to the observance of all Christian virtues; and therefore it ought to be of great influence in suppressing the contagion of wicked societies. Let, therefore, this holy sodality be strengthened

by a daily increase. Amongst the many benefits to be expected from it will be the great benefit of drawing the minds of men to liberty, fraternity, and equality of right; not such as the Freemasons absurdly imagine, but such as Jesus Christ obtained for the human race and St. Francis aspired to: the liberty, We mean, of *sons of God,* through which we may be free from slavery to Satan or to our passions, both of them most wicked masters; the fraternity whose origin is in God, the common Creator and Father of all; the equality which, founded on justice and charity, does not take away all distinctions among men, but, out of the varieties of life, of duties, and of pursuits, forms that union and that harmony which naturally tend to the benefit and dignity of the State.

Restore Catholic Guilds

35. In the third place, there is a matter wisely instituted by our forefathers, but in course of time laid aside, which may now be used as a pattern and form of something similar. We mean the associations or guilds of workmen, for the protection, under the guidance of religion, both of their temporal interests and of their morality. If our ancestors, by long use and experience, felt the benefit of these guilds, our age perhaps will feel it the more by reason of the opportunity which they will give of crushing the power of the sects. Those who support themselves by the labor of their hands, besides being, by their very condition, most worthy above all others of charity and consolation, are also especially exposed to the allurements of men whose ways lie in fraud and deceit. Therefore they ought to be helped with the greatest possible kindness, and to be invited to join associations that are good, lest they be drawn away to others that are evil. For this reason, We greatly wish, for the salvation of the people, that, under the auspices and patronage of the Bishops, and at convenient times, these guilds may be generally restored. To Our great delight, sodalities of this kind and also associations of masters, have in many places already been established, having, each class of them, for their object to help the honest workman, to protect and guard his children and family, and to promote in them piety, Christian knowledge, and a moral life. And in this matter We cannot omit mentioning that exemplary society, named after its founder, St. Vincent. which has deserved so well of

the people of the lower order. Its acts and its aims are well known. Its whole object is to give relief to the poor and miserable. This it does with singular prudence and modesty; and the less it wishes to be seen, the better is it fitted for the exercise of Christian charity, and for the relief of suffering.

Special Guidance of Youth

36. In the fourth place, in order more easily to attain what We wish, to your fidelity and watchfulness We commend in a special manner the young, as being the hope of human society. Devote the greatest part of your care to their instruction; and do not think that any precaution can be great enough in keeping them from masters and schools whence the pestilent breath of the sects is to be feared. Under your guidance, let parents, religious instructors, and priests having the cure of souls, use every opportunity, in their Christian teaching, of warning their children and pupils of the infamous nature of these societies so that they may learn in good time to beware of the various and fraudulent artifices by which their promoters are accustomed to ensnare people. And those who instruct the young in religious knowledge will act wisely, if they induce all of them to resolve and to undertake never to bind themselves to any society without the knowledge of their parents, or the advice of their parish priest or director.

A Call to Prayer and Action

37. We well know, however, that our united labors will by no means suffice to pluck up these pernicious seeds from the Lord's field, unless the Heavenly Master of the vineyard shall mercifully help us in our endeavors. We must, therefore, with great and anxious care, implore of Him the help which the greatness of the danger and of the need requires. The sect of the Freemasons shows itself insolent and proud of its success, and seems as if it would put no bounds to its pertinacity. Its followers, joined together by a wicked compact and by secret counsels, give help one to another, and excite one another to an audacity for evil things. So vehement an attack demands an equal defense—namely, that all good men should form the widest possible association of action and of prayer. We beseech them, therefore, with united hearts, to stand together and unmoved against the advancing force of the sects; and in mourning and supplica-

tion to stretch out their hands to God, praying that the Christian name may flourish and prosper, that the Church may enjoy its needed liberty, that those who have gone astray may return to a right mind, that error at length may give place to truth, and vice to virtue. Let us take as our helper and intercessor the Virgin Mary, Mother of God, so that she, who from the moment of her conception overcame Satan, may show her power over these evil sects, in which is revived the contumacious spirit of the demon, together with his unsubdued perfidy and deceit. Let us beseech Michael the prince of the heavenly angels, who drove out the infernal foe; and Joseph, the spouse of the Most Holy Virgin, and heavenly Patron of the Catholic Church; and the great apostles, Peter and Paul, the fathers and victorious champions of the Christian faith. By their patronage, and by perseverance in united prayer, We hope that God will mercifully and opportunely succor the human race, which is encompassed by so many dangers.

38. As a pledge of heavenly gifts and of Our benevolence, We lovingly grant in the Lord, to you, Venerable Brethren, and to the clergy and all the people committed to your watchful care, Our Apostolic Benediction.

39. Given at St. Peter's in Rome, the twentieth day of April, 1884, the 6th year of Our Pontificate.

LEO XIII, POPE.

DISCUSSION CLUB OUTLINE

By Rev. Gerald C. Treacy, S.J.

I

The world is divided into two kingdoms, the Kingdom of God and the Kingdom of Satan. The Kingdom of God is the Catholic Church. Its citizens strive to serve God and live up to the teachings of Christ. The Kingdom of Satan is made up of those who refuse to obey God's Eternal Law, following the sad example of their leader and of our first parents, Adam and Eve.

St. Augustine described these two kingdoms as two cities, saying: "Two loves built two cities; the love of self reaching even to contempt of God, an earthly city, and the love of God reaching to contempt of self, a heavenly city." There has always been conflict between these two cities. The battle has at times been intense, at other times less intense. Today (1884) however the forces of evil, the earthly city, Satan's Kingdom, seem to be battling with united vigor under the leadership of a world-wide organization called the Freemasons.

These forces no longer work in secret. They have openly declared war on God, and call for the destruction of the Church. Their aim is the dechristianizing of the nations of the world. It is Our duty to sound a note of warning in this critical hour, and to meet the enemies of God with every resource at Our command. A Christ's Vicar on earth, it is an obligation of Our office to see that the Kingdom of Christ not only holds the line against the onslaughts of Satan's cohorts, but that it carries on to victory, spreading its saving message of Divine Truth farther and farther into the confines of the world.

Our predecessors, the Roman Pontiffs, were quick to detect the enemies of God, as soon as they appeared out of the darkness of their secret councils, and they were prompt to warn the nations and their leaders against the snares and the deceits that were craftily being planned for the destruction of Christendom. The first warning given by Clement XII in 1738, was repeated by every Pope down to the recent days of Pius IX.

For as soon as the real meaning of Masonry appeared from the publication of its official documents, laws, rites and commentaries, the Apostolic See condemned the principles of this sect, as contrary to God's law, dangerous alike to religion and the State, and forbade Catholics to join the lodges under penalty of excommunication. The Masons replied by falsely accusing the Sovereign Pontiffs of acting unjustly and without due moderation. A few members of the Order however admitted the right and justice of the Papal attitude. Moreover many government heads concurred with the policy of the Popes, and several States branded masonic teachings as hostile and dangerous to public peace and order.

The rightness of the Popes' condemnation has been proved by the course of events. Wherever rulers of States allowed Masonry to flourish against the warning uttered by the Vicar of Christ, the result has been that the lodges have grown strong enough in 150 years to take over the powers of government. And the harm foreseen by Our predecessors against religion, public peace and the State itself is today evident to all thinking men. Indeed today we have reason to fear not for the Church whose foundation is strong with divine power, but for every State where masonic power prevails.

For these reasons as soon as We became Head of the Church, We determined to attack this evil with all Our authority. We have already pointed out the falsity of masonic teachings on several occasions. In exposing the fallacies of Socialists and Communists, We have explained the true Christian teaching on domestic life, and We have described the Christian ideal of political government. It is Our present purpose to explain the teachings and practices of Masonry, and to bring to light its power for evil that the poisonous progress of this fatal plague may be stopped (1-9).

QUESTIONS

Into what two kingdoms is the world divided?
Name the leaders and the followers in these kingdoms.
What two loves form these kingdoms?
What is Masonry's relationship to these two kingdoms?
How does Pope Leo state the masonic plan?
What did the Pope say of his immediate duty in the year 1884?
What had the previous Popes done?
Where did the Popes get their information on Masonry?
What did this information reveal about Masonry?
How did Masonry answer the charge of the Roman Pontiffs?
What was the reaction of some members of the masonic sect and of some governments to the statements of the Pontiffs?
What has been the result of the growth of Masonry on the Church and State?
Has the State more to fear from Masonry than the Church?
What is Pope Leo's plan in this encyclical?

II

There are several secret societies differing in name, yet one in principle and purpose. They are all centered around Freemasonry. For they stem from it and revert back to it. They now meet openly and express their views through their own press. Nevertheless they follow the wrong policies of secret societies. They hide their real objectives even from a good number of their own membership. The names of their leaders are carefully hidden. Candidates are obliged to promise under oath to reveal nothing in regard to the membership, the subjects discussed at the meetings, the passwords and the plans. Like the Manichees of old, they strive to have no witnesses to their actions but their own members. They often mask their real designs by claiming to be literary societies concerned only with the advance of culture, or else societies devoted to the welfare of the poor. Even if these objectives were aimed at, they would not be their chief aim. Absolute and blind obedience is exacted of the candidate toward his leaders. Punishment for disobedience is severe, and often means death.

An organization that binds men to slavery such as this, forcing them to obey the arbitrary will of another under pain of death, is evidently opposed to justice and cannot but produce evil. "A good tree cannot produce bad fruit, nor a bad tree good fruit." And the fruit produced by Masonry is evil and bitter. For it is nothing less than the overthrow of the Christian social and political order, and the substitution of a new world-order founded on Naturalism.

We are not speaking of the aims of *individuals* who belong to the masonic society or its allied associations. For there are a great many members who do not know the real purpose aimed at by these groups. These men are to be blamed however for joining societies under secret oath, without investigating their aim and purpose. Nor do We pronounce judgment on masonic accomplishments. We judge it on its official teachings.

Masonry is founded on Naturalism. That means that human nature and human reason are supreme, and that there are no truths revealed by God that men are bound to believe. The Naturalist denies the authority of the Catholic Church as God's Voice upon earth and against that Church the hatred of Naturalism is chiefly aimed.

Following the tenets of Naturalism, Masonry advocates the complete exclusion of the Church from any civic influence, banns all cooperation between Church and State, and relegates religion and the Church to the realm of private and personal life. Not only does Masonry disregard the Church, but by speech and writing it attacks the very foundation of the Church. It denies the God-given rights of the Church, and restricts its liberty of action at every opportunity. It seeks by laws, apparently not hostile but in reality so framed, to hinder the apostolate of the clergy, to curtail the ownership and administration of Church property, and to disperse the Religious Orders (10-14).

QUESTIONS

Are the different secret societies united with Masonry in their aims?

Mention some things that these societies keep secret.

What promises must a candidate make on joining a secret society?

How does Masonry resemble the old sect of the Manichees?

Mention some methods of concealment used by Masonry.

What penalty may be imposed by Masonry on a disobedient member?

The obedience exacted by Masonry is against justice. Prove.

What does the Pope say is the ultimate purpose of Masonry?

Is the Pope speaking of individual members or of the ideas of Masonry?

The new order of life planned by Masonry is built on Naturalism. Explain.

Do all members of Masonry, and of its affiliated societies approve all its aims?

According to Pope Leo how is Masonry to be judged?

State the fundamental doctrine of Naturalism.

What does Naturalism teach regarding man's duties to God?

Prove that Masonry wishes to carry out the teachings of Naturalism.

Does Masonry merely advocate disregarding the Church?

Briefly state Masonry's policy regarding the Church.

III

The attacks of Masonry are directed especially against the Vicar of Christ. First the Pope was deprived of his temporal possessions, the bulwark of his liberty. Then he was unjustly forced to live in a condition that can be aptly called unbearable; and now what was long said secretly in the lodges is openly proclaimed, namely that the Papacy must be utterly destroyed.

If the candidate for Masonry is not required to abjure his religion, this is not done out of reverence for religion, but to teach the great modern error that religion is a matter of indifference and that all religions are alike. That teaching once accepted would destroy all religion and especially the one true religion given by Christ to His Church.

Naturalism denies the existence of God, the spirituality and immortality of the human soul, truths which may be learned by the light of reason alone. Following this error, Masonry allows its votaries to accept the existence of God or to reject it. The Supreme Architect of the universe, the masonic term for God, may mean anything or nothing.

With this basic truth of God's existence weakened, all other truths that human reason can arrive at, soon disappear; namely that God created all things, that His Providence rules the universe, that the soul does not die but is destined for an eternal life. With the vanishing of these truths, private and public morality disappear. For they are the foundation on which all morality rests. Remove God from human life and there is no motive for right living, no meaning to justice or injustice.

Masonry favors the teaching of natural morality and argues for an education for youth without any religious belief. The results of this may be seen today wherever the right idea of Christian education has been abandoned, due to masonic influence, in the breakdown of morality both public and private (15-19).

QUESTIONS

How has Masonry acted toward the Roman Pontiff?

To Masonry all religions are alike. Explain the consequence of this.

What does Naturalism teach about the existence of God, the spirituality and immortality of the soul?

Does masonic membership require a belief in God's existence?

What other important truths hinge on the truth of God's existence?

State the sources and principles of all justice and morality.

What is the masonic plan for teaching morality?

Name the effects that have followed, when this plan has been carried out.

What is the attitude of Naturalism and Masonry toward God's revelation?

What is their position regarding the struggle between passion and reason?

What means do they use to lead men to a life of pleasure?

IV

As human nature has been weakened and wounded by Original Sin, it is more inclined to vice than to virtue, to the law of passion than to the rule of reason. Naturalism and Masonry both deny this sad truth. Their teaching exaggerates the power of natural virtue, and holds that it alone is strong enough to secure the reign of justice. They will not admit the need of constant struggle to curb our passions. And so by every agency of propaganda, the press, the theatre, the arts, men are allured to a life of mere pleasure. Man's happiness, they teach, is of the earth, earthy. The light of heaven is blacked-out from human vision. Once men have become the slaves of their passions, they will be easily induced by crafty and daring leaders to carry out any task commanded them. There have been some among the masonic fraternity who have openly advocated this perverting program.

In regard to domestic life, the following are the tenets of Naturalism. Marriage is a kind of commercial contract, revocable at the will of the contracting parties. The State has complete jurisdiction over the marriage bond. In education no religion is to be taught as certain, but it is to be left to the youth when he comes of age to select whatever religious belief he chooses.

Masonry endorses these falsehoods and endeavors to incorporate them into civil law. In many countries, nominally Catholic, laws have been passed making civil marriage alone lawful, in others divorce is legalized. So that the time is fast approaching when the marriage contract will be entered into with the idea of ending it as soon as the contracting parties so determine. Masonry also attempts to control the education of youth, and mold it to its own godless pattern. So the Church is allowed no share in education, and in many places Masonry has succeeded in placing it entirely in the hands of laymen, and has banished from moral teaching all mention of man's duties to God.

The political theories of Naturalism sponsored by Masonry hold that man is the source of all rights, that all men are in every sense equal, that no man has the right to command another, and that those holding authority in the State depend completely on the popular will and may be deposed at its pleasure. God is excluded from the State and all forms of religion are on an equal footing. This is the kind of State that Masonry aims at, and for some time past it has used all its power and resources to accomplish this aim. This of course is preparing the way for Red Radicalism which wants the destruction of all ranks in society, the abolition of property, and common ownership of all goods.

What Masonry means and what it aims at is clear from the above summary. Its chief dogmas are against human reason. It is the height of folly and impiety to attempt to destroy the Religion and Church established by God, and to reestablish paganism. It is horrible to think that a concerted effort is under way to repudiate all the benefits that our Lord and Saviour has gained for individuals, families and for civil society. In this insane and wicked endeavor we may almost see the vengeful hatred of Satan for Christ (20-25)

QUESTIONS

What advantage would Masonry reap if all men followed its teachings?

Enumerate Naturalism's teachings on marriage and education.

How does Masonry regard the influence of the Church in education?

Enumerate Naturalism's political doctrines on sovereignty and obedience.

In sponsoring these doctrines Masonry is helping the arrival of what radical social order?

What does the Pope say of the chief dogmas of Masonry?

What would the effect of these dogmas be on Christian civilization?

V

Masonry by joining with the subversive forces that are striving to undermine the foundations of justice and honesty, and to establish an era of license that they call liberty, is only helping forward the ruin of Christian civilization. Domestic and civil society are in grave danger at this time. For the sacred character of marriage, as God established it, is constantly attacked by those who would destroy its permanence, thereby depriving the wife and mother of her dignity, and the children of protection and security. At the same time there is spreading a dangerous teaching that would exclude God from any part in civic affairs, just as if He did not exist. Even the agans did not so act, for they believed it would be easier to have a State without a foundation than a State without God.

The State like the individual comes from God, and the State like the individual is by nature obliged to honor and worship God. For God in creating man put into his nature an urge to live together with his fellow men, that is to establish the State. So it is as wrong for the State to shut God out of its life, as it is for the individual to do this. As the State comes from God, and the State cannot exist without authority, so the authority in the State comes from God. He then who wields the legitimate authority in the State is the representative of God, and provided he rules justly, his authority cannot be rejected by the citizens whenever they please.

All men are equal, for God has created all men and given them a common destiny. They are equal in the rights and duties that belong to them as creatures and children of God. Men are not equal in abilities as they differ from one another in mental and physical power. As star differs from star in beauty, so does man differ from man in disposition, temperament and character. It is both foolish and unreasonable to imagine that men may be leveled down to a common equality as citizens of the State. Just as in the human body there is dissimilarity of parts and diversity of functions all contributing to the unified whole, so in the body politic or the State there are differences and distinctions between man and man, office and function, all contributing to the common welfare which is the end or object of the State.

The errors We have described are a menace to all States. For if God is not honored and His Laws respected, if lawful authority is scorned and subversive doctrines encouraged, a complete overturn of the social order will necessarily follow. Many groups of Socialists and Communists advocate this. Freemasonry is in accord with it. If their efforts are not successful it is because the sounder part of men refuse to be drawn into these secret societies, and because the power of God's true religion still prevails.

It would be well if all men could see the origin of the evils that threaten us. For we are facing a deceitful and crafty enemy who wins over peoples and their leaders by flattery. Masonry pretending friendship for the rulers of States, tries to make of them allies for the destruction of Christianity. Falsely accusing the Church of endeavoring to infringe upon the rights of rulers, Masonry has attained to great political influence within many governments. With this power it is ready to bend rulers to its will and is prepared to depose those rulers who will not carry along government according to masonic dictates.

Masonry in like manner deceives the people with flattery and falsehood. For it promises them liberty and prosperity if they will follow its lead, and declares the Church and the rulers of States responsible for the people's poverty. It urges the people to attack

[29]

both the Church and the civil power. And wherever the deluded people have followed the masonic lead they have found their last state worse than their first. For there is no social order that can bring peace and prosperity to the people unless it is a Christian order.

The Church is wrongly accused of derogating from the civil power because she directs men to obey God above all. The true teaching of the Church is Christ's teaching: "Render to Caesar the things that are Caesar's and to God the things that are God's." In maintaining that all authority is from God, the Church gives dignity to civil authority, and inspires in citizens true loyalty and obedience. Mother of men, and friend of peace, the Church is the great helper of all classes, teaching that justice must be mingled with kindness, equity joined to authority, moderation to legislation. She maintains the sacredness of each individual's rights, the tranquillity of order in the State, and the duty of the State and of private charity to relieve the needs of the poor. It would then be political wisdom on the part of rulers, and a measure redounding to their own welfare on the part of the people to join with the Church in repelling the masonic conspiracy instead of joining with Masonry to destroy the Church (25-30).

QUESTIONS

How does Masonry agree with and how does it differ from Paganism?

What is the true teaching of the origin of human society?

Are States as well as individuals bound to honor and worship God?

What is the origin of authority in the State?

Why is it a duty to obey lawful authority?

Explain the real equality and inequality of men.

Show how the members of the social body resemble the members of the human body.

If the errors mentioned by Pope Leo are not checked, what effects will follow?

What is the plan of Socialists and Communists, and how does Masonry regard it?

Why has this plan not succeeded so far?

How has Masonry won the sympathy of civil rulers?

How will Masonry use its influence in civil affairs?

What has been Masonry's strategy towards rulers and the people?

How have the people fared under masonic influence?

How does the teaching of the Church add dignity to civil authority?

How does this teaching give a motive for civic obedience?

What should political wisdom dictate regarding this teaching?

Whatever the future may be, it is Our present duty to stem the evils of Masonry. Our best remedy is in that divine religion which is hated and feared by the masonic sect. So whatever Our Predecessors have decreed against Masonry, and whatever they have enacted to deter or withdraw men from secret societies of this kind, We ratify and confirm by all Our Apostolic authority. And We plead with all Christians not to depart in the least from what the Apostolic See has commanded in this matter.

We ask Our fellow-bishops to join with Us in Our efforts to rid the State of this poison which is creeping through its veins. We ask the bishops, each in his own diocese, first to unmask Masonry and let it be seen for what it is. In sermons and pastoral letters the people should be taught the deceits used by these secret societies to entice men into their ranks. Their evil theories and actions should be pointed out. What Our Predecessors have said, We repeat: Let no Catholic become a Freemason if he values his Faith and his eternal salvation. Let no man be deceived by any pretense on the part of the lodges. If it seems that they demand nothing that is contrary to religion and morality, it must be realized that the principles and objects of these secret societies are vicious and criminal, and so it is unlawful to join them or help them in any way.

There is need too of giving the people by sermons and writings a better knowledge of the teachings of their Faith, so that they will be protected against the assaults of error. Clergy and laity should unite in deepening their knowledge of and love for the Church. Thus equipped they will not be deceived by the appeal of the secret societies.

We earnestly urge the spread of the Third Order of St. Francis as an antidote to the spread of secret societies. For this Order wins men to the imitation of Christ by the practice of the virtues He taught, and inspires them with love for His holy Church. Herein men will learn true liberty, equality and fraternity, which Christ Himself obtained for mankind and to which the gentle St. Francis aspired. It is the liberty of the sons of God, by which men are freed from the slavery of Satan, sin and disordered passions. It is the fraternity of God the common Creator and Father of all. It is the equality founded on justice and charity, that out of a variety of duties and offices in the State, unifies all for the common good.

Workmen's associations should be formed under the guidance of the bishops and priests, modelled on the ancient guilds, to look after the spiritual and temporal welfare of workers. Catholic societies are the best answer to the dangerous allurements of secret societies. It is good to know that a start has been made in forming such groups. And We wish to commend here the work and aim of the St. Vincent de Paul Society in its apostolate among the needy.

We strongly urge bishops and priests to safeguard the education of youth. Warn the young against the evil that lies hidden in secret societies, and urge them never to join any society without consulting their parents and spiritual guides.

All our efforts will be in vain, however, without divine help. Masonry and its evils must be met by a world-wide front of men of good will, united in action and prayer. We must all pray God that Christian truth may prevail over error, Christian virtue over vice, that the Church of Christ may enjoy liberty, and that her wandering children may quickly return to her fold. Invoking the aid of our Blessed Mother, St. Joseph, St. Michael, St. Peter, St. Paul and the great Fathers and Defenders of the Faith, our prayers will move the mercy of God to help the children of men, beset as they are by so many dangers (30-39).

QUESTIONS

The Pope advises priests and bishops to meet Masonry in what manner?

The Pope characterizes Masonry's principle and object in what two words?

How does Pope Leo regard the actions of his Predecessors towards Masonry?

What does the Pope say to the Catholic about joining a masonic lodge?

The Pope proposes a united front against Masonry. Who are to form it?

What does Pope Leo say of the Third Order of St. Francis?

Explain the liberty, fraternity and equality that is true.

What does the Pope say of the ancient guilds of workers?

What Church society does the Pope commend for work among the needy?

To whom does the Pope ask the bishops to devote special care?

What methods are to be used by teachers of the young and what counsel given?

State in your own words the Pope's appeal for a united front of action and prayer.